Beautiful YORKSHIRE

John Potter

Consultant editor Melvyn Jones

MYRIAD

LONDON

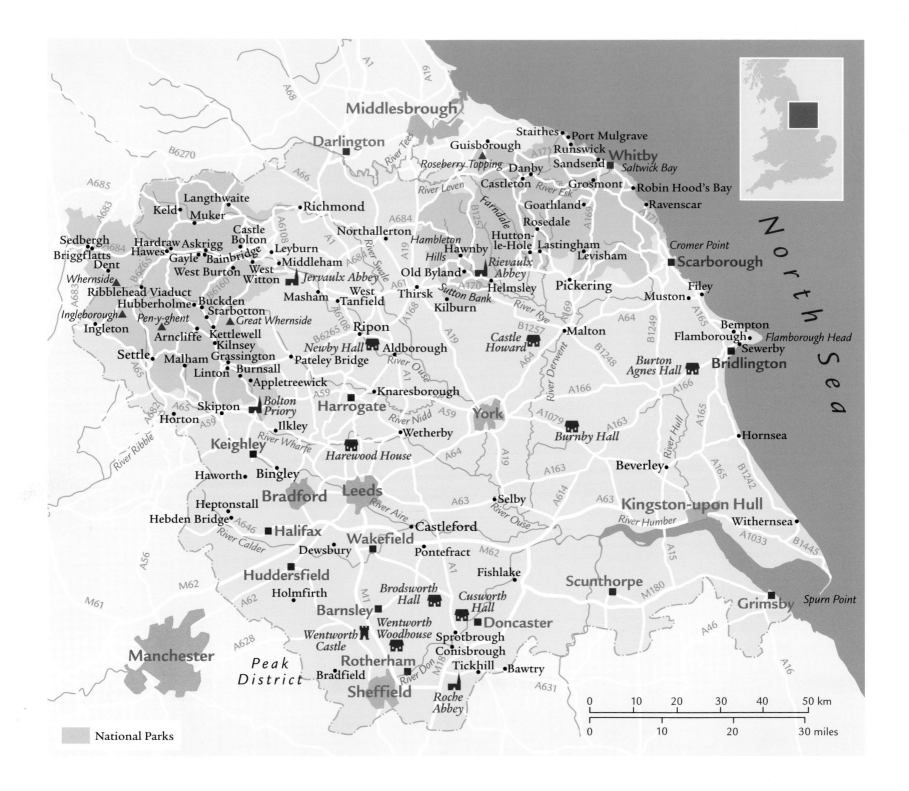

National Parks

0 10 20 30 40 50 km
0 10 20 30 miles

First published in 2008 by Myriad Books Limited
35 Bishopsthorpe Road, London SE26 4PA

Photographs copyright © John Potter
Text copyright
© Myriad Books

Consultant editor Melvyn Jones

ISBN 1 84746 133 6
EAN 9 781 84746 133 9

Designed by Jerry Goldie Graphic Design
Map artwork Stephen Dew

Printed in China

www.myriadbooks.com

CONTENTS

INTRODUCTION

The historic county of Yorkshire, stretching from the river Tees in the north to the river Humber and the borders with Derbyshire, Nottinghamshire and Lincolnshire in the south and from the high Pennine peaks in the west to the North Sea coast in the east is a county of superlatives. It is the biggest ancient county in Great Britain and has long been said to cover more acres (3,669,510 at the last count) than there are words in the Bible. HV Morton on his motoring tour of England in the 1920s – *In Search of England* – was of the opinion that it was not so much a county as a country: "God's Own Country", as it has been labelled by generations of Yorkshiremen and women. Containing two national parks, the Yorkshire Dales and the North York Moors, and parts of another (the Peak District) it is also the greenest county in the country.

And the county has given so many things to the world: Yorkshire pudding, Yorkshire relish, Yorkshire tea, Yorkshire mixture (delicious boiled sweets), Wensleydale cheese, forced rhubarb and Harrogate toffee, to name but a few. Yorkshire people throughout history have also made major impacts: Eric Bloodaxe, Robin Hood (definitely not from Nottinghamshire!), Guy Fawkes, Captain James Cook, William Wilberforce, the Brontë sisters, Henry Moore, Judi Dench, Michael Parkinson, the list is almost endless.

But it is Yorkshire's beautiful landscape that is the county's greatest gift. It is a many-layered landscape, a natural landscape, fashioned by the hand of nature over millions of years and a cultural or human landscape fashioned over thousands of years. The great variations in geology, relief and altitude, from nearly 3,000ft (914m) to sea level, have resulted in human beings adapting to their natural surroundings in a myriad of ways. The result is a landscape of infinite variety and beauty. A rural landscape, covering hill and dale, criss-crossed by drystone walls or old hedgerows, with ancient woodlands hanging on hillsides, and with the population clustered in isolated farmhouses, hamlets and villages, often with a medieval parish church, and urban landscapes of every type from ancient market towns, with their minster churches and often protected in the past by stone-built castles, to fishing ports tucked into small bays along the North Sea coast and major towns and bustling cities.

John Potter's camera has captured brilliantly the natural landscapes, from the great power and majesty of the rugged peaks of Ingleborough and Pen-y-Ghent, the broad sweeps of the heather-covered Bradfield and Emley Moors and the powerful waterfalls of East Gill Force and Scalebow Force, to the limestone pavements of Malham, the windswept heights of Sutton Bank and the magnificent high, vertical cliffs at Bempton and Flambrough. He has been equally successful in capturing the human landscapes whether he has been concerned with the farming landscapes of the Yorkshire Dales and the North York Moors, country houses and their parks and gardens as at Castle Howard or Brodsworth Hall, religious buildings such as Rievaulx Abbey or York Minster, great transport innovations such as the Ribblehead Viaduct or the Humber Bridge, the streetscapes of small towns like Richmond, Thirsk or Beverley or the grand cityscapes of Bradford, Leeds and Sheffield. Turn the page and begin your virtual journey through John Potter's *Beautiful Yorkshire*.

Right: located in the the upper Holme valley, the Digley reservoir overlooks Holmfirth

WEST YORKSHIRE

West Yorkshire is a landscape of contrasts. There are great differences between the physical landscapes of the west and centre where the Pennines reach a height of 1,725ft (526m) and are cut into by the upper reaches of the valleys of the Wharfe, Aire and Calder and their tributaries that made the region such a fulcrum of growth and change during the Industrial Revolution, to the relatively low-lying eastern lowlands on the edge of the Vale of York. There are contrasts, too, in the urban landscapes of the great cities of Leeds and Bradford, the major towns of Halifax, Huddersfield and Wakefield, and the small towns such as Keighley, Pontefract and Wetherby. But all is not urban and industrial; there are small interesting villages such as Heptonstall, Howarth and Heath and great houses such as Harewood, Temple Newsam and West Bretton set in their landscaped parks.

Emley Moor & Bradford Alhambra

Two contrasting West Yorkshire scenes: Emley Moor (left) with its towering TV transmitter and (right) the Alhambra Theatre in Bradford. The first TV transmitter on Emley Moor was erected in 1956, then it was rebuilt in 1964 and then again in 1969 after storm damage. At 1,064ft (330m) this tapering reinforced concrete tower is the tallest free-standing structure in the UK. The Alhambra Theatre was built in 1914 for the musical impresario Frank Laidler, the "King of Pantomime". It was restored in 1986 after suggestions that it might be demolished and a car park built in its place.

Central Leeds

Leeds, the commercial and financial capital of Yorkshire, has many fine buildings. Dominating the heart of the city is Leeds Town Hall, constructed between 1853-58 and designed by Cuthbert Brodrick, the Hull architect. It is a solid and confident flagship of a proud Victorian city, topped by a magnificent domed clock tower (right and below) rising to 225ft (68m). The city's coat of arms, on Leeds Bridge (below), dating back to the 1660s, contains three stars from the coat of arms of the first mayor, Thomas Danby, owls from the coat of arms of the first alderman, Sir John Savile, and a fleece, reflecting the wool industry's role in Leeds' history. The gilded owl, bottom left, stands beside the Civic Hall (1931-33) in Millennium Square. More ancient than the Civic Hall is St Peter's, Leeds parish church (second right). Built between 1837-41, it replaced the medieval church at a cost of £30,000. It was denied cathedral status in the late 19th century.

Modern development

New building development is a hallmark of Leeds. Above is No 1 City Square, completed in 1998, a 12-storey block with a black granite base, white limestone upper storeys and external lift shaft. Leeds Waterfront (left) was the city's dockland area at the termini of the Aire and Calder Navigation and the Leeds and Liverpool Canal. By the 1960s this area was rundown and partially derelict. It has now been transformed. Existing warehouses have been converted into apartments and offices and new riverside apartments and office buildings have been constructed.

Leeds market

A new market hall (left) was built in 1904 by architects John and Joseph Leeming at the junction of Kirkgate and Vicar Lane replacing the original market hall of 1857. A disastrous fire in 1975 destroyed two-thirds of the interior and another fire in 1992 set back restoration work that had begun in 1991. Now the exterior stonework has been repaired, the domes rebuilt and shop units and stalls replaced or repaired in their original style. Other surrounding Victorian market buildings have been restored and the open market has been provided with new stalls and a central market square created.

Leeds retail and commercial

Leeds is a bustling retail, commercial and financial centre. The treasures of the retail quarter are the covered shopping arcades: Thornton's Arcade (1877-8), Grand Arcade (1897), Queen's Arcade (1899) and County Arcade (1898-1904). The County Arcade (far left) presents the visitor with one of the most beautiful shopping environments in the city. It is 394ft (120m) long and has mahogany shopfronts with curved glass windows, separated by pilasters and columns of Siena marble above which are balustraded balconies crowned by an arched cast-iron roof. Park Row (left) lies at the commercial heart of the city and was described in the late 19th century as "the Pall-Mall of Leeds". Clocks seem to festoon the city: they are found not only at the Town Hall and at the city's churches but also in the shopping arcades and (below) at the Civic Hall.

Kirkstall Abbey

The ruins of Kirkstall Abbey (below) lie just three miles north-west of Leeds city centre. This abbey was founded in 1147 by monks and lay brothers from Fountains Abbey but they did not move to Leeds until 1152. It is believed that the church was completed within 25 years. In 1890 the site was bought from a private owner and presented to Leeds Corporation who undertook some building repairs before opening it as a public park in 1893.

Temple Newsam

Temple Newsam (right) is a grand 17th century country house that derives its name from the Knights Templar who held the manor from 1155 to 1312. The present house was built in brick in the Jacobean style in the 1620s or 30s by Sir Arthur Ingram. The house and more than 900 acres of gardens and parkland were acquired by Leeds Corporation in 1922 and became a museum, park and golf course. There are beautiful gardens, a farm and a rare breeds collection.

Roundhay Park

This 373-acre public park (above and left), the largest in Leeds, was opened in 1872. It was first mentioned in the 12th century when it was a deer park (hay = hedged deer enclosure) owned by the de Lacy family and part of the boundary ditch still survives in the north-east corner. The park was bought in 1871 by the Lord Mayor of Leeds and a group of associates who then sold it to the Corporation. It was slow to develop as a popular attraction and was nicknamed "The Great White Elephant" until the electric trams reached it in the early 1890s allowing for the first time the ordinary folk of Leeds to reach it quickly and cheaply. Among its attractions are the 33-acre Waterloo Lake which is fed from the north by a series of cascades and waterfalls, the smaller Upper Lake, a sham castle, the Canal Gardens, the Alhambra Garden, Monet Garden and the Coronation House (now Tropical World).

CANAL GARDENS

These ornamental gardens were formed from a walled kitchen garden built c.1816 for Thomas Nicholson of Roundhay Park. Inheriting the estate in 1833, his stepbrother Stephen added the canal, 350 by 34 feet, spanned by two rustic bridges and terminating in an arbour.

Harewood House

This magnificent country house, the home of Earl and Countess Lascelles, was built by the York architect John Carr between 1759 and 1772 on the instructions of Edwin Lascelles whose father had made his fortune in the ribbon trade, from his position as collector of customs in Barbados and his directorship of the East India Company. The interiors were the work of Robert Adam and much of the furniture is by Thomas Chippendale. In the 1840s the south façade of the house was remodelled by Sir Charles Barry, the architect of the Houses of Parliament. The grounds were laid out by Lancelot "Capability" Brown. To the south of the house is an ornamental garden with intricate flower-beds, fountains and herbaceous borders. Still the home of the Lascelles family, Harewood is one of Yorkshire's major tourist attractions.

Pontefract

The beautiful octagonal tower of St Giles' church stands sentry over Pontefract, and is visible for miles around. St Giles mainly dates from the Georgian era, but the site has been a centre of religious worship since the 12th century. The church interior contains splendid stained-glass windows some of which are dedicated to long-serving vicars and prominent Pontefract families. Between 1868-9, the Earl of Harewood built the beautiful Sanctuary Chapel. Overlooking the market square stands the Buttercross. It was gifted to the town by Solomon Dupier who vowed to erect a covered market cross if his wife and three daughters survived the smallpox they had all contracted. In the event they did recover but all four lost their sight; nevertheless, in 1734 the Buttercross was built and provided shelter for the country women who brought their dairy produce to market well into the 20th century. Pontefract Castle (right), built in 1070, was reduced to ruins during the Civil War.

Wakefield

An inland port on the river Calder, Wakefield's prosperity stemmed from the wool trade. The Cathedral of All Saints (below) has a fine musical tradition and boasts Yorkshire's tallest spire at 247ft (75m). The old Wakefield toll bridge is home to the medieval St Mary's Chantry chapel, one of only six bridge chapels built in Britain. Today Wakefield is famous for the Yorkshire Sculpture Park at Bretton Hall. Set within beautiful parkland, thousands of visitors come each year to be inspired by exhibits of modern and contemporary sculpture in a superb natural setting. The collection includes works by Henry Moore, Barbara Hepworth and Eduardo Paolozzi.

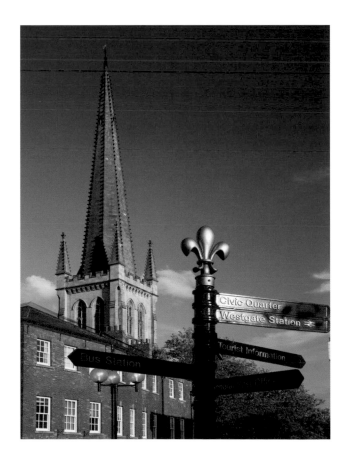

Bradford

Two of Bradford's surviving medieval buildings are Bolling Hall (above) and the Cathedral (left). Now a museum, and just a mile from the city centre, Bolling Hall gives visitors an insight into the lives and times of the two families for whom it provided a home over five hundred years. During the Civil War the household supported the Royalist cause, and Bolling Hall was a stronghold during the "Siege of Bradford". The Cathedral stands to the east of the city centre. Its tranquil garden belies its stirring history – in 1642-3, during the Civil War, the tower was bombarded by the army of Charles I. Its interior contains stained-glass by William Morris, and a plaque to famous "Bradfordians" – including the inventor and industrialist Samuel Lister and the writer JB Priestley.

Bradford Town Hall

The magnificent neo-Gothic Town Hall (left) dates from 1873; the scale of the building reflects Bradford's prominence and its ambition as a commercial centre of trade, worthy of being ranked with other cities such as Liverpool and Glasgow. Re-named City Hall in 1965, its frontage overlooks Centenary Square and is graced with sculptures of British monarchs, including Oliver Cromwell – an echo of Bradford's role in the Civil War.

Cliffe Castle Museum, Keighley

Set amidst beautiful parkland, the mansion at Keighley (above) is not a medieval castle but a Victorian one – created by the textile magnate Henry Isaac Butterfield who transformed the earlier Cliffe Hall into the enchanting Cliffe Castle in 1878. In 1950 Sir Bracewell Smith, a local man, bought the castle and presented it to the people as a museum; today it is a treasure trove of natural history and geology, local artefacts, furniture and stained glass – including a set of William Morris panels made for the Temple Street Methodist Chapel in Keighley in 1921.

Five Rise Locks

The engineers who built Britain's canals in the early days of the Industrial Revolution had to overcome many challenges, including the differing levels of the countryside through which they drove this new mode of transport. Completed in 1777, Five Rise Locks at Bingley on the Leeds and Liverpool Canal raises the level of the waterway by 59ft (18m). On the Yorkshire side of the Pennines, as the canal rises out of Airedale, there are, within a 16 mile stretch, three double locks, four staircase locks of three locks each, and then the Bingley Rise – originally called the Bingley Great Lock.

Cow and Calf

Up on the famous Ilkley Moor, two rocky outcrops of millstone grit have long been known as the Cow and Calf rocks; with their steep slopes these and other outcrops are popular with climbers of all abilities. Ilkley Moor is part of Rombalds Moor which rises to over 1,600ft (396m) in places. It is rich in archaeological remains including cairns, barrows, hut circles and "cup and ring" carvings. The moor has long been a favourite with walkers – from the top there are glorious views over Wharfedale.

Haworth

The photograph above is of the Brontë Parsonage Museum at Haworth; the one to the right is of the town centre. When the Rev Patrick Brontë brought his family to live at the parsonage in Haworth in 1820 the village was little more than a cluster of stone cottages clinging to a steep hill, with the church at the top of the street and the moors stretching into the distance. Today the fame of this extraordinary family has spread far and wide and visitors descend on the town and the museum in their thousands. The Parsonage is full of paintings, books and papers that belonged to the Brontës and the rooms have been lovingly restored to convey to visitors what life was like for the parson and his family of writers. The village retains its Victorian air with cobbled streets, an old-fashioned apothecary's shop, antiquarian booksellers and antique shops. A network of paths radiates from the village into the surrounding countryside. Walkers can make their way to the Brontë Falls and Top Withens on the moors above Haworth. The setting of this farmhouse, now in ruins, is thought to have inspired Emily Brontë's *Wuthering Heights*.

Halifax

In a valley seven miles south-west of Bradford, Halifax is the capital of Calderdale. The town owes its prosperity to the wool trade and its town hall (right) was designed by Sir Charles Barry, the architect of the Houses of Parliament. The Piece Hall (centre right), completed in 1779, contains more than 300 rooms built around an open quadrangle; it was here that handloom weavers living in outlying cottages brought their "pieces" of woollen cloth to sell. The Wainhouse Tower (left) was built for John Edward Wainhouse to carry the smoke and fumes produced by his dye works out of the Calder valley. At 253ft (77m) high it is one of Calderdale's best-loved landmarks. The beautiful Victoria Theatre (right) was built in 1901 originally as a concert hall. It was converted into a theatre in 1960 and is currently being refurbished.

Hebden Bridge and Heptonstall

Eight miles west of Halifax, the beautiful town of Hebden Bridge grew rapidly in the 18th and 19th centuries as a result of the wool trade, the fast-flowing waters of the river Calder providing power for the mills in the area. The wool trade brought the Rochdale Canal (above), completed in 1804; this canal is particularly popular as its route crosses the Pennines, giving wonderful views of the breathtaking scenery of Calderdale. The original settlement of Hebden Bridge centred on the hilltop village of Heptonstall; the magnificent view (right) is of Hebden Bridge from Heptonstall while the bowling green below is at Heptonstall with Stoodley Pike in the distance. At 110ft high (36m) the Stoodley Pike monument was constructed in 1856 to commemorate the end of the Crimean War. It was built on the site of an earlier monument which marked the defeat of Napoleon, but this was struck by lightning in 1854 and collapsed.

Heptonstall's churches

The ancient hilltop village of Heptonstall is home to two churches, which both share the same graveyard. The ruined church of St Thomas à Becket dates from 1256 and was dedicated to Becket, the archbishop who was murdered on the orders of the king in 1170 and became a symbol of resistance to authority. In 1847 this medieval chapel was partially destroyed in a great storm. A new church, in the Victorian Gothic style, was built; dedicated to St Thomas the Apostle it was consecrated in 1860 and contains the 11-sided font from the old chapel; its bells too have incorporated those from the ruined church and ring out over the hills and valleys, calling the congregation to prayer. The Quaker plaque (right) reflects the fact that Quakers and other Non-Conformists flourished in Calderdale; John Wesley preached in the village on a number of occasions.

Huddersfield

The West Riding town of Huddersfield boasts 1,660 listed buildings – only Bristol and Westminster have more. One of the town's most famous sons was the Labour prime minister Harold Wilson. His statue (right) was erected in 1999 and graces St George's Square in front of the railway station. The magnificent town hall (below) doubles as a concert hall and is home to the renowned Huddersfield Choral Society. It

was designed by John H Abbey and was built in two stages between 1875 and 1881. It is "classic Italianate" in style, defined by the rounded heads to the windows and the symmetrical design. Inset: a decoration on one of the cast iron pillars supporting the open air market's roof.

Railway station

Huddersfield station (above) was constructed in 1847-48. It has been called "a stately home with trains in it". Its classical façade is 416ft long and it is supported by eight

68ft high columns. It is decorated with the coat of arms (left) of the Huddersfield and Manchester Company which built the station.

Right: the view towards Stoodley Pike from Heptonstall.

Holme Valley

The Digley reservoir is one of a number in the upper Holme valley overlooking Holmfirth. Immediately to the west is the smaller Bilberry reservoir which burst its banks in 1852, causing the death of 81 people in the valley below.

Castle Hill

The hill fort at Almond-bury near Huddersfield, seen here from Farnley Tyas is made up of a series of Iron Age and medieval earth-works. The flat-topped hill has been the site of Chartist rallies as well as prize-fighting. The Victoria or Jubilee tower was added in 1899 to celebrate Queen Victoria's Diamond Jubilee two years earlier.

Holmfirth

Three miles south of Huddersfield, Holmfirth is situated at the confluence of the rivers Holme and Ribble. This picturesque Pennine town developed rapidly in the 16th century thanks to the burgeoning cloth industry and its local slate and stone mines. Now the town and its surrounding countryside are best known as the setting for the long-running television series *Last of the Summer Wine*. Thousands of tourists flock to the area each year to enjoy the scenery and hoping to identify locations used in the

series. Sid's Café (right) in the centre of the town, a watering hole familiar to all *Last of the Summer Wine* viewers, is now a place of pilgrimage for fans. Next door to the character Nora Batty's fictional house in the series, is the Summer Wine exhibition (below) which combines the Wrinkled Stocking Tea Room and a re-creation of the character Compo's home.

THE DALES

The Yorkshire Dales National Park which straddles the Pennines is an area of outstanding natural beauty where pretty villages nestle amidst the typical Dales scenery of drystone walls and barns or close to stark limestone escarpments. The grandeur of the Three Peaks, the scenic Settle to Carlisle railway line and the outstanding limestone scenery of Malhamdale are all to be found in this region.

Swaledale and West Burton
These attractive stone barns (above), so typical of the northern Dales, are situated between Aygill and Thorns Green close to the road that links Thwaite to Keld in Upper Swaledale. There is a disused quarry in the valley bottom and beyond the lower slopes of Kisdon Hill rise sharply to a summit of 1,637ft (499m). West Burton in Wensleydale (right) is famous for the magnificent West Burton Falls, just east of the village, a popular location for artists and photographers.

Keld

The small village of Keld (left) nestles snugly at the head of Swaledale, its pretty stone cottages clustered around a tiny square. The hamlet is the crossover point of the Coast-to-Coast and Pennine Way footpaths. The name of the village derives from the old Norse word "keld", meaning spring and the nearby river Swale is fed by many small becks which flow down from the surrounding fells. Ten minutes' stroll from the village, just north of the Pennine Way, where the long-distance footpath crosses East Stonesdale, is East Gill Force (below).

Langthwaite

The picturesque village of Langthwaite (left) is the largest settlement in Arkengarthdale, the most northerly of Yorkshire's dales. Its stone cottages huddle together haphazardly along Arkle Beck, three miles north-west of Reeth. The cosy and welcoming Red Lion was used extensively in the filming of the television series *All Creatures Great and Small*. The "Waterloo" church of St Mary constructed in 1817 was typical of many churches built after the French Revolution to counteract atheism and free thinking. It is traditional to lock the church gates during weddings and for local children to gather outside – the gates are only unlocked and the wedding party freed when money is tossed to the waiting children!

Richmond

The capital of Swaledale, Richmond (above) is dominated by its castle keep, part of the massive castle built by Alan the Red of Brittany, a trusted supporter of William I. Richmond ranks among the most beautiful towns in England, with many elegant Georgian houses, cobbled streets and pretty cottage gardens. At the centre of the impressive market place is the 12th century chapel of the Holy Trinity, now used as the regimental museum of the Green Howards. In 1788, Samuel Butler, a local actor and manager, built the Theatre Royal, a small and beautiful Georgian theatre, which is still in use today. Situated in the middle of Richmond at the bottom of the market place and overlooked by Millgate House, a beautiful Georgian townhouse, is a unique and beautiful south-facing walled garden, open to the public between April and October.

Gunnerside

The beautiful windswept fells and attractive patchwork of fields, drystone walls and barns along the valley bottom make this part of Swaledale (left) a favourite with visitors. In early summer the wildflower meadows are a vibrant sea of colour, and a delight to walk through. Gunnerside Gill runs through the tiny village of Gunnnerside and meets the river just below the King's Head Inn.

Muker

The pretty village of Muker (right) sits proudly above Straw Beck at the head of Swaledale about one mile east of Thwaite. The colourful east window of St Mary the Virgin depicts the scenery around the village including the river Swale and Straw Beck, together with 23 horned sheep – a reference to Psalm 23. *The Lord is my Shepherd.*

Kisdon Hill

The limestone mass of Kisdon Hill (bottom) stands proud at the head of Swaledale. This viewpoint looks south towards Muker.

Bainbridge

Set in the heart of Wensleydale, Bainbridge (below) has a wide village green with ancient stocks. The village is overlooked from the east by the remains of a Roman settlement. The horn hanging in the Rose and Crown Inn on the village green is a reminder of the time when the great forest of Wensleydale dominated the area. Each evening the Bainbridge horn-blower would sound his horn to guide forest workers and travellers back to the village. The custom continues to this day – every year the horn is sounded at 10pm from September 27 (the Feast of the Holy Rood), until Shrove Tuesday.

Hawes

Looking towards the busy market town of Hawes (left) known as the "little capital" of Upper Wensleydale. Hawes sits comfortably between high fells at the head of the dale and is Yorkshire's highest market town. The lively Hawes Livestock Auction Mart has weekly sales and livestock produce from this area is famed far and wide for its quality. Hawes is home to the Wensleydale Creamery where the famous Wensleydale cheese is produced and to the Dales Country-side Museum. Just six miles away at Garsdale station, the Settle-Carlisle railway line links the Eden Valley and Ribblesdale with the Three Peaks.

Hardraw

The village of Hardraw lies among spectacular scenery (below) almost at the foot of Buttertubs Pass – a link road over the fells from Wensleydale to Thwaite in Swaledale. The village is a stopping off point for walkers on the Pennine Way or those embarking on the ascent of nearby Great Shunner Fell, a bleak and remote summit which, at 2,349ft (716m) offers (in good weather!) spectacular views of the Three Peaks, Wensleydale and Swaledale.

Gayle

Just south of Hawes, Gayle (above) is sited at the foot of Sleddale. Duerley Beck cascades over a series of limestone steps in the centre of the village before rushing below a packhorse bridge. Early spring showers often swell the beck causing a torrent of foaming water to race past the rows of terraced cottages sited on the bank (left).

Aysgarth Falls

Situated seven miles west of Leyburn, Aysgarth is best known for the spectacular waterfalls (right) on the river Ure that cascade down a series of large limestone steps. Riverside walks link the Upper, Middle and Lower Falls which are all within a mile of each other. The best view of the Upper Force is from the 16th century bridge in the centre of the village.

Askrigg

Just one mile north-east of Bainbridge on the northern side of Wensleydale, Askrigg (above) is a tiny settlement best known as the setting for the popular television series *All Creatures Great and Small*. Above the village sits Askrigg Common and beyond it the unmistakable form of Addlebrough. Askrigg was a former medieval market town and is now a haven for walkers and daytrippers.

West Burton Falls

One mile south of Aysgarth at the northern end of Bishopsdale, the pretty, unspoiled village of West Burton has a large village green surrounded by traditional Dales' stone cottages. The annual May Fair, held on the green, draws large crowds. To the east of the village, the glorious West Burton Falls (right), known locally as Cauldron Falls, are best seen from the footbridge at the north end of the village. After heavy rainfall, the falls quickly change from a quiet and picturesque waterfall to a raging and forceful torrent.

Castle Bolton

The small village of Castle Bolton, five miles west of Leyburn, is dominated by Bolton Castle (above). This massive fortress has loomed over Wensleydale since 1379 and is one of the country's best preserved castles; Mary Queen of Scots was imprisoned here in 1568 and 1569. In the middle of the village is a wide green and St Oswald's, the attractive 14th century church which nestles in the shadow of the castle.

Middleham

Another local village dominated by its castle is Middleham (above and left) situated just two miles from Leyburn between Coverdale and Wensleydale. This impressive defensive structure was built around 1170 by Robert Fitz Randolph during the reign of Henry II. The massive central keep has 12ft (3.5m) thick walls and is one of the largest in England. The countryside around Middleham is a centre for the training of racehorses.

West Witton

Four miles west of Leyburn, West Witton (above) sits in the lee of Penhill which dominates the skyline in this part of Wensleydale. This photograph was taken from the minor road that climbs steeply out of the village to the south and up past Penhill Farm to Melmerby. The parish church of St Bartholomew (right) was originally Saxon, and possibly dates from the sixth century.

Leyburn

An intense game in progress at Leyburn Bowling Club (left). Leyburn is the main commercial and market town for Lower Wensleydale. It is well-known for fabulous views over Wensleydale from Leyburn Shawl, a grassy terrace high above the valley to the west of the town which is easily reached from Shawl Terrace at the top of Market Place. The town is linked to nearby Middleham by a suspension bridge, built in 1829 – one of the first ever to be constructed – over the Ure.

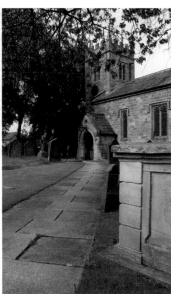

Dent

The pretty village of Dent is actually in Cumbria, four miles south-east of Sedburgh, although it lies within the Yorkshire Dales National Park. The white-painted cottages are very Cumbrian in character in contrast to the warm natural stone buildings usually found in the lower Yorkshire Dales. The view above looks north-west from just below Combe Scar and shows the Howgill Fells in the distance; the view (top right) shows the vista to the east towards Aye Gill Pike from the other side of the village.

Brigflatts

The Quaker Friends Meeting House (left) at Brigflatts, half a mile from Sedbergh was built in 1675. At this time, the village was a thriving community of around 75 people who ran their own cottage industry relying on flax weaving. In 1881 a raised wooden floor was fitted to allow water from the village pond to flow through the meeting house without wetting the feet of the congregation. The poet Basil Bunting (1900-1985) is buried in the Quaker graveyard in the village.

Ingleborough

The second highest of the Three Peaks, Ingleborough is pictured right shrouded in mist on a bitterly cold winter's day looking from Runscar Scar below Runscar Hill. It owes its distinctive shape to a broad cap of millstone grit on top of a broader plateau of limestone. The lower slopes have many complex and cavernous caves and potholes where streams suddenly disappear. Gaping Ghyll, where Fell Beck runs into the largest-known underground chamber in Britain, offers expert potholers a real challenge.

Kingsdale

To the north of Ingleborough in Kingsdale are the rocks known as the Cheese Press Stones (left) so-called because they are similar to the stones used to press cheese into shape.

Ingleton

This pretty market town is surrounded by dramatic limestone scenery both below and above ground. The Ingleton Waterfalls (below) are on the rivers Twiss and Doe. The late Victorian church of St Mary (right) lies close to pretty woolworkers' cottages (above).

43

Horton in Ribblesdale

Six miles north of Settle, Horton (left) is one of the most popular potholing centres in the region and the starting point for the 25-mile Three Peaks Walk which includes the summits of nearby Pen-y-Ghent, Ingleborough and Whernside. The walk should be completed in less than 12 hours. The Pen-y-Ghent café in Horton provides much more than large pots of refreshing tea; it's also the spot where Three Peaks' walkers clock in and out to register their progress on this arduous trek. For lovers of an even greater challenge, the famous Three Peaks Race takes place each year at the Horton Gala.

Ribblehead Viaduct

The 72-mile Settle-Carlisle railway line is one of the most picturesque in Britain and runs through Ribblesdale offering dramatic views of Whernside and Pen-y-Ghent. Constructed in the 1870s, the line was renovated and reopened in 2000. The magnificent 24-arch Ribblehead Viaduct (below) to the north-west of Ribblehead station is seen here from Runscar Hill.

Pen-y-Ghent

The enticing view of Pen-y-Ghent (above) from Dale Head on the remote Stainforth to Littondale road, part of the long-distance Pennine Way footpath. The Pennine Way follows this dead-end road for some distance and then goes up and over the summit at 2,277ft (694m) and then down into the village of Horton.

Scalebar Force

In a deep wooded ravine just outside Settle, on the road to Kirkby Malham, Scalebar Force (right) is a cascading waterfall in a deeply wooded valley. During wet weather, the pretty rivulet changes into a raging torrent. The word "force", a Yorkshire dialect word for a waterfall, comes from the old Norse word "fors", which is sometimes corrupted to "foss".

Malham

Malhamdale is immensely popular with visitors because of its unique limestone landscape developed over millions of years, first by glacial erosion and then by the effects of wind, rain and frost. Three of the best examples – the limestone cliff at Malham Cove, Malham Tarn and Gordale Scar are sited behind the attractive village of Malham (right), five miles west of Settle. Above the Cove lies Malham pavement (below), where hundreds of limestone blocks or "clints" are indented by deep fissures or "grykes".

Arncliffe

This pretty hamlet (left) lies at the heart of lovely Littondale and is the largest of its four settlements which also include the village of Litton and the small hamlets of Halton Gill and remote Foxup. Arncliffe has a central wide open green, surrounded by mellow stone cottages and farm buildings. Littondale was the setting for Charles Kingsley's *The Water Babies* and it was also chosen originally as the setting for the long-running and very popular ITV series *Emmerdale*. Several large porched barns indicate that this is still very much a typical Dales' working community.

Foxup

This tiny hamlet (right) is the most remote of the settlements in Littondale. This viewpoint is from Low Bergh looking north over Foxup towards Ber Gill and Eller Carr Moss. Cosh Beck and Foxup Beck join just below the houses and run quickly downhill to form the river Skirfare just before Halton Gill.

Halton Gill

A village with a spectacular setting (below) Halton Gill is sheltered by Plover Hill, Cow Close Fell and Horse Head Moor. The stone houses and farm buildings of the village sit beside the infant river Skirfare with its attractive packhorse bridge.

Hubberholme

This tiny village (above and below) on the Dales Way four and a half miles from Kettlewell is famous for its beautiful church and atmospheric pub. The church of St Michael and All Angels has choir stalls and pews made in 1934 by Robert Thompson, the "Mouseman" of Kilburn, who left the distinctive carving of one of these small creatures on all of his furniture. The churchyard is the resting place for the ashes of the novelist JB Priestley, who loved the village.

Great Whernside

Wharfedale and Nidderdale run parallel to each other in a north-west to south-easterly direction. From Buckden to Bolton Abbey, Wharfedale has magnificent upland scenery. The rugged fell of Great Whernside (right) dominates the skyline east of Buckden. Not to be confused with Whernside (one of the Three Peaks further west) it reaches a height of 2,310ft (705m) and creates an abrupt change from the lush pastures below. The long boulder-strewn ridge gives extensive views across Nidderdale to the east and westward to Wharfedale.

Starbotton

Just two miles north of Kettlewell, Starbotton (below) was almost completely swept away in the great flood of 1686 due to its low-lying position next to the river Wharfe. The village lies under Buckden Pike, which at 2,302ft (701m) is a stiff challenge for the hillwalker.

Kettlewell

In the shadow of Great Whernside, Kettlewell is popular with potholers and walkers. Its buildings are clustered close to Cam Beck near where it joins the river Wharfe. Low winter sunshine and a light scattering of snow reveals the distinctive pattern of drystone walls and field barns, so typical of the area (below). These fields lie just south of the village; the long-distance footpath, the Dales Way, which links Ilkley to Windermere, runs along the valley bottom.

Buckden

The annual Buckden Pike Fell Race (right) starts and finishes on the gala field in Buckden each year. Buckden is a perfect base to explore the glorious scenery of Wharfedale. Starting from the village, a popular triangular walk of approximately seven miles takes in the small hamlets of Cray, Yockenthwaite and Hubberholme. In spring, the wild-flower meadows by the river Wharfe (left) are a colourful and vibrant highlight of the walk. Close to the summit of Buckden Pike is a well-known memorial to the Polish crew of an aircraft that crashed here in 1942.

51

Wharfedale

Running from north to south, Wharfedale is one of the Dales' longest and most beautiful valleys. The unique and stunning landscape of Wharfedale is revealed in this view (above) from Rowan Tree Crag looking towards Hartlington Hall and Kail Hill, just east of Burnsall.

Kilnsey

Three miles north of Grassington, this tiny village (left) nestles in the shadow of Kilnsey Crag, a dramatic peak much loved by climbers. Kilnsey Park Trout Farm, shown here, offers fly fishing and a nature trail. The annual Kilnsey Agricultural Show is a much-loved Wharfedale event.

Linton

One mile south of Grassington, this characterful village (right) has a large irregular village green which slopes eastwards towards the banks of Linton Beck. Riverside paths run along the side of the beck which is crossed by a packhorse bridge, a road bridge, a clapper bridge, stepping stones and a weir – making this an ideal spot for a leisurely walk.

Grassington

At the heart of Wharfedale, Grassington has a long history as a market town – a tradition that is carried on to this day in the cobbled square at the heart of this attractive settlement. Every Christmas the town is transformed into a Victorian village with shopkeepers and local people dressed in Dickensian costumes. After dark, braziers are set up around the square to add to the atmosphere.

Appletreewick

This peaceful Wharfedale village four miles south-east of Grassington rests on a steep slope overlooked by the craggy summit of Simon's Seat. The main street is lined by ornate and characterful cottages with High Hall at the top of the hill and Low Hall at the bottom. The original owner of High Hall was Appletreewick's most famous inhabitant, Sir William Craven. Known as "Dick Whittington of the Dales" he was a local farmer's son who was sent to London to make his fortune and eventually became Lord Mayor of the city in 1610. Loyal to his roots, Willam returned to Appletreewick and rebuilt High Hall.

Burnsall

Ten miles north-west of Ilkley, Burnsall (above) is famous for the massive five-arched bridge which spans the river Wharfe. Every August, the village hosts England's oldest fell race.

Valley of Desolation

This aptly named area (left) is a tributary valley to Wharfedale branching off from Strid Wood. Posforth Gill runs through the valley and is fed by a number of small springs and gills on Barden Fell. There are some very picturesque waterfalls along this pleasant wooded ravine and a delightful walk up through the valley leads to the rocky outcrop of Simon's Seat, which towers over the quiet and unspoiled village of Appletreewick.

Gouthwaite Reservoir

Looking down across the lush green pastures of Nidderdale (above) to Gouthwaite Reservoir in the far distance from Thrope Plantation. The plantation is located one and a half miles from Lofthouse close to the minor road that links Lofthouse to Masham. The area around the reservoir is a bird-lover's paradise and there are a number of viewing points along its shore from which "twitchers" can observe birds of prey and a variety of waders. Gouthwaite Reservoir and nearby Angram and Scar House reservoirs were constructed in the early part of the 20th century to supply Bradford with water.

Bolton Priory

This beautiful Augustinian priory (left) is a stone's throw from the village of Bolton Bridge five miles west of Skipton. The beautiful ruins are immensely popular with visitors who can also enjoy a picnic along the banks of the nearby river Wharfe. Close by, the river gushes in a thunderous cascade though a narrow chasm – known as "the Strid". Further upstream, along a nature trail, is Barden Bridge and the beautifully sited Barden Tower, which was built in 1485 by Lord Henry Clifford.

Pateley Bridge

At the heart of Upper Nidderdale is the small town of Pateley Bridge (above) which is packed with dark gritstone buildings, narrow meandering streets and cobbled alleyways leading to quaint courtyards. The Nidderdale Museum in the town offers a view of early Dales' life. Around the town are steep fells with panoramic views across Nidderdale. A plaque in the High Street marks the start and finish of the Nidderdale Way – a circular route of 53 miles that takes in most of the spectacular sites in the area.

West Tanfield

The village of West Tanfield (above) overlooks the river Ure on the eastern edge of the Dales. The village skyline is dominated by both the Marmion Tower, a 15th century gatehouse noted for its great arch and oriel window and St Nicholas' church. The church contains the beautiful alabaster tomb of Sir John and Lady Elizabeth Marmion. Lady Marmion may have lived in the Tower after the death of her husband, using it as a "Lady Castle" or dower house.

Masham

Pronounced "Massum", this peaceful small market town (right) is situated in Lower Wensleydale midway between Ripon and Leyburn. Masham's attractive cobbled market-place – the largest market square in Yorkshire – is surrounded by elegant Georgian houses and tea rooms and is overlooked by the beautiful spire of St Mary's church. The square was the site for annual sheep fairs where over 80,000 animals would be sold. Today, this tradition is continued on a smaller scale each September. The town boasts two famous breweries – Theakstons and Black Sheep. The Masham Steam Engine and Fair Organ Rally (below) takes place in July.

Jervaulx Abbey

Situated between Masham and Leyburn are the ruins of this atmospheric Cistercian abbey (below). Dating from 1156 the abbey fell into ruin after the Dissolution in 1537. Enough remains of the ivy-covered crumbling walls to remind us of the simple yet austere lives of the "white monks". A weathered effigy of the abbey's great benefactor, Hugh Fitzhugh, stands in the grounds. The site is closely identified with Wensleydale cheese since it is thought that the monks perfected the recipe.

VALE OF YORK

This large region of low-lying, undulating countryside stretches from the river Tees in the north to Selby in the south, a distance of more than 50 miles, and from the eastern edge of the Yorkshire Dales in the west to the Howardian Hills and the Yorkshire Wolds in the east. Underlain by glacial deposits it is a rich agricultural area with hay meadows along the river floodplains and large fields elsewhere intensively cultivated for arable crops. There are scattered small woods and larger conifer plantations on sandy soils. The farmhouses and villages are built of a distinctive mottled brick with pantile roofs. The Vale of York is an important transport corridor containing the A1 and A19 trunk roads and the East Coast Main Line railway connecting London with Edinburgh. The region includes the busy market towns of Northallerton, Knaresbrough and Thirsk, the elegant spa town of Harrogate and the cathedral cities of York and Ripon.

Kilburn White Horse & Castle Howard

Early morning frost covers the fields (above) close to the village of Coxwold in the beautiful Vale of Mowbray. On the distant escarpment is the White Horse of Kilburn. This striking chalk figure in the shape of a horse was carved into a hillside overlooking the Vale of York in 1857 and can be seen from 40 miles away. One of Britain's finest historic houses, Castle Howard (right) 25 miles north-east of York was built to a design by John Vanburgh from 1699-1712 and is set amongst magnificent parkland. This opulent residence is, along with Blenheim near Oxford, regarded as a masterpiece of English Baroque architecture. It gained fame with television audiences when it was used as the setting for *Brideshead Revisited*, the 1981 adaptation of Evelyn Waugh's celebrated novel.

York

Sited at the confluence of the rivers Ouse and Foss, this ancient city has had a turbulent history. Founded by the Romans, it suffered Viking invasion, was ravaged by William the Conqueror and became a major Royalist stronghold during the English Civil War. The city's eventful past is reflected in the many important historic buildings packed within its city walls: attractions such as York Minster (right), the narrow medieval streets around its core which include the famous Shambles, together with the Jorvik Viking Centre and the York Castle Museum have made the city one of the most popular tourist destinations in the UK. York has the longest and best-preserved town walls in Europe and there are 45 towers and four gateways (or "bars") at intervals along its length. A walk along the top of the wall is an ideal way to view the city.

York Minster

The largest Gothic cathedral in northern Europe, York Minster is the seat of the archbishop of York, the second highest office in the Church of England. There has been a church here since 627; work on the current Minster began in 1220 and was not completed until 1472. York Minster is famous for the Great East window, completed in 1408, the largest expanse of medieval stained glass in the world. The view on the right looks up to the ceiling of the Transept Tower.

Lendal Bridge

This elegant iron bridge (below), with stone towers at either end, was built by Thomas Page in 1863. It is one of nine bridges over the river Ouse in York.

Roman York

The city of York was founded by the Romans in AD71. Then known as Eboracum, the city was the capital of Roman Britain. Outside the Minster is a statue of Constantine who was proclaimed Roman Emperor in York in 306 when his father died. This act plunged the entire Roman Empire into a long and bloody civil war.

Clifford's Tower

This distinctive stone fortification (below) in Tower Street is all that remains of the 13th and 14th century keep of York Castle. In 1190, a mob began to attack the city's Jewish residents and, fearing for their lives, 150 people took refuge in the wooden tower which then occupied this site. The militia laid siege to the tower for several days, when a fire broke out. All of the Jews inside the tower were killed either by the flames or having decided to commit suicide rather than surrender themselves to the mob.

Bootham Bar

The statue of local artist William Etty (right) stands in front of the City Art Gallery looking towards Bootham Bar with York Minster in the distance. Large parts of the city wall still exist along with four gatehouses or "bars". In peacetime the bars were designed to restrict traffic and make the work of collecting tolls easier; in times of war, they helped to protect against potential armed invaders. Bootham Bar was partially rebuilt in the 14th and 18th centuries but it still has stonework dating back to the 11th century.

York Abbey

The ruins of St Mary's abbey (above and left) lie to the west of York Minster in the Yorkshire Museum gardens. Close to the city centre, this is the ideal spot for visitors and office-workers to relax and enjoy the beautiful gardens. The Benedictine abbey was founded in 1055 and was once the richest Benedictine establishment in the north of England. In 1539, the monastic community was disbanded and the abbey destroyed during the Dissolution. All that remain today are the north and west walls and St Mary's tower in the north-west corner of the abbey. The abbey precinct wall forms part of the town wall of York.

York attractions

One of York's highlights is the Shambles (above), a meandering medieval street leading up to the Minster. Today it is filled with souvenir shops; in the Middle Ages it was home to many butchers (the name Shambles comes from the Anglo-Saxon word *Shammels* or *Fleshshammels* – meaning an open-air slaughterhouse). Most of the buildings along the Shambles are medieval but there are also some outstanding Tudor half-timbered houses. The Shambles is so narrow that some of the upper floors of the houses almost touch. In the grounds of the National Railway Museum is an observation wheel (left) which gives spectacular views over the city. York's historic Guildhall (above left) on the banks of the Ouse behind the Mansion House, dates from the 15th century.

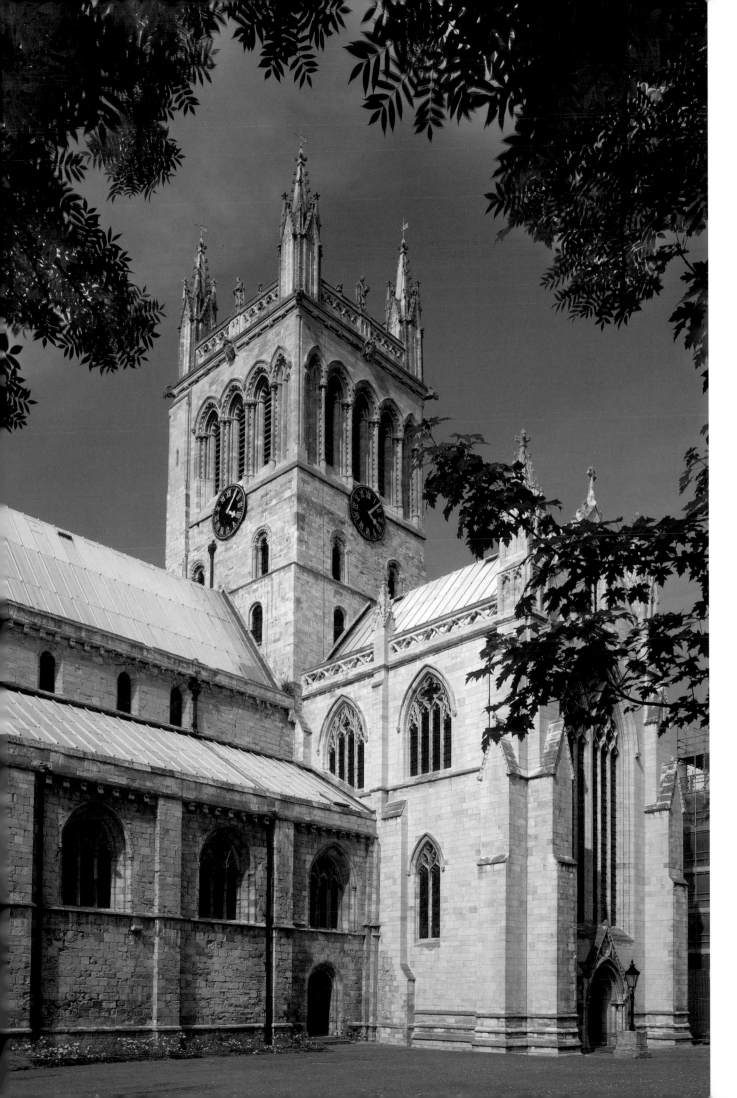

Selby

This attractive market town lies 12 miles south of York along the river Ouse. In the past, Selby was an important shipbuilding centre and harbour thanks to the Selby Canal which linked the town with Leeds. The town is dominated by Selby abbey (left) founded by the Benedictines in 1069, and modelled on Durham cathedral. It is one of the largest parish churches in Britain and is famed for the 14th century Washington window which features the heraldic arms of the ancestors of George Washington, first president of the USA. The design has three red stars above two red bands and is said to be the model for the American flag.

Harrogate

The first mineral spring was discovered at the Tewitt Well in this North Yorkshire town in 1571. By the 18th century, Harrogate had become a fashionable spa to rival Bath and Buxton. The Royal Pump Room (left) has been converted into a museum telling its story. It is possible to visit the sulphur wells where more than 15,000 people would come for treatments. Next to the museum is Valley Gardens (below) where many of the wells were found. Today it is one of Harrogate's gorgeous public parks.

Mercer Gallery
Originally built in 1806 as Harrogate's first spa building, the Mercer (above) is now home to the district's superb collection of fine art. The building includes the beautifully restored Promenade Room.

Tea rooms
Bettys and Taylors opened its first "continental-style tea room" on Cambridge Circus (left) in 1919. Since then the company has started another Bettys Tea Room in Harrogate at Harlow Carr and in a number of other Yorkshire towns.

Harlow Carr
The 58 acre RHS garden at Harlow Carr (right) in Crag Lane rivals Wisley in Surrey. It contains an Alpine house and kitchen garden.

Knaresborough

The beautiful town of Knaresborough grew up around the steep sides of the gorge of the river Nidd. This has been a strategic point for centuries and during the Middle Ages Knaresborough was firmly established on the royal circuit. The Norman castle (right) was used as a hideout by the four knights who murdered Thomas à Becket in 1170. It was badly damaged during the Civil War when the Parliamentarians besieged the Royalists here; a Parliamentary decree in 1646 ordered its destruction and many buildings in the town centre are constructed from "castle stone". The castle's remains are open to the public and its grounds are used as a performance space – in particular for events during the Knaresborough Festival every August. In 1851 the dramatic viaduct across the gorge was completed.

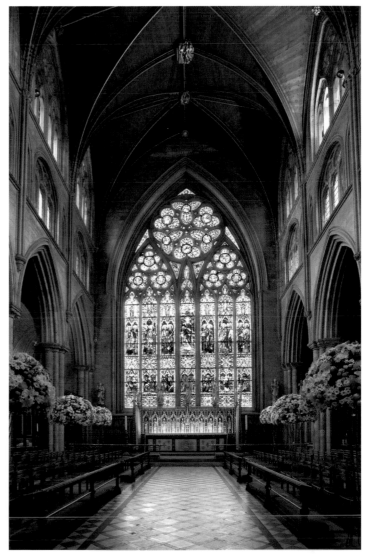

Ripon Cathedral

The small city of Ripon lies to the north of Knaresborough on the banks of the river Ure. The cathedral was founded on the ruins of St Wilfred's Abbey and the present building dates from the 12th century. Its western front and towers are fine examples of early English church architecture. The Decorated nave (above) was built in the 15th century.

Newby Hall

Sir Christopher Wren guided the design of Newby Hall (left), near Ripon, built in 1697. Since 1748 it has been home to the Compton family, whose ancestor William Weddell bought the property and enlarged it during the 1760s. The interior was remodelled by a variety of architects, including Robert Adam, and it is an exceptional example of 18th century interior design. The present grounds were laid out in the 1920s, with herbaceous borders and a dramatic broad grass walk leading down to the river Ure. In 2007 Newby Hall was used for the filming of the television adaptation of Jane Austen's novel *Mansfield Park*. Still privately owned, the house and gardens are open to the public from March to September.

Northallerton

This market town stands in the centre of the Vale of York and has long been an important centre of communications between north and south. Due to its strategic position, Northallerton has often served as a base for armies in times of war. During the Civil War the town was a Royalist stronghold and in 1641 Charles 1 stayed at Porch House (below), one of Northallerton's oldest houses built in 1584. Later the town was a resting place for the Duke of Cumberland's troops in their campaign against the Jacobites. Today the town has a thriving market and useful shops – Barker's department store with its distinctive clock over the entrance (right) has been trading for over 125 years. All Saints church, at the northern end of the High Street, has pews made by the famous workshop of Robert Thompson, the "Mouse Man of Kilburn", and decorated with his trademark emblem (top left). The pretty village of Danby Wiske lies five miles to the north-west. The beautiful parish church (below) stands amidst the fields on the edge of the village and dates from the 12th century.

Thirsk

This lively town lies south of Northallerton overlooking the Hambleton Hills and close to the North York Moors. Thirsk has a long tradition of flower displays and is a frequent award-winner of the Yorkshire in Bloom competitions. The town is built around an impressive medieval market square (above) which hosts a twice-weekly open-air market. The church of St Mary (above right) is over 500 years old and the nave has a beautiful timbered roof. One of the stained-glass windows in St Anne's chapel (right) was created from the jumbled fragments of other windows in the church during a major 19th century restoration project. A plaque (left) marks the birthplace of Thomas Lord who founded Lord's cricket ground; his home now houses Thirsk Museum. Thirsk's most famous modern resident was the author James Herriot (the pen name of James Alfred Wight) who practised as a vet at 23 Kirkgate, now home to the World of James Herriot Museum. Herriot's semi-autobiographical stories – known as the *All Creatures Great and Small* novels – tell of the eventful life of a small-town vet living and working on the edge of the North York Moors.

Summer shows

Agricultural shows, large and small, have been the lifeblood of agricultural communities, and great social occasions, throughout the county for generations. The grandest of these is the Great Yorkshire Show held over three days at the show ground on the edge of Harrogate. It incorporates international show jumping, marching bands and the Great Yorkshire Cheese & Dairy Show. Equally important are the local shows that are eagerly looked forward to throughout the year and are organised by the show committees in minute detail over many months. The Malton Show (above), for example, has now been going for more than 120 years. In the 1880s when the show began it was a place for farmers and other country folk to meet, exchange stock, and discuss new ideas and for the womenfolk to trade homemade preserves. Today the show has increased greatly in size and includes, besides the traditional competitions for best horses, cattle and sheep, cooking and crafts, such things as a grand parade, sheep dog trials, an owl sanctuary and vintage tractors. The Ripley Show (left), held in the grounds of Ripley Castle, includes falconry displays and racing terriers.

Aldborough and Boroughbridge

This long-established local show (above, left and centre) was first held more than 90 years ago. The cattle breeds at the 2006 show included Charolais, Blonde d'Aquitaine, Limousin, Dexter, Aberdeen Angus, Shorthorn and Highland. Dogs too play an important part, with gun dog displays and demonstrations of agility. A horticultural section has prizes for the best sweet peas and flower arranging. And it is not only agricultural shows that attract large crowds. The classic car rallies held at Newby Hall (left) are great crowd-pullers, whether exhibiting Wolseleys, Fords or MGs. In 2003 the Harrogate MG Club held their 18th rally at Newby Hall and attracted 2,000 MG cars of every age and model.

NORTH YORK MOORS

One of the finest upland landscapes in Britain, the North York Moors include the north-east corner of Yorkshire stretching northwards from the Vale of Pickering to the border with County Durham and from the Hambleton and Cleveland Hills in the west to the coast. A large part of the region has been designated as a national park. With its heather-clad moorland, fertile dales and characterful villages and market towns, this region has one of Yorkshire's most beautiful and captivating landscapes. Dales penetrate the moorlands; from the North Sea coast, for example, Eskdale runs deep inland and Farndale and Rosedale penetrate northwards from the Vale of Pickering. These dales within the moorlands have always been very important. They have heavy clay soils that are variable in quality, but in such barren surroundings they have a crucial role and contain almost all the village settlements.

Blakey Ridge and Sutton Bank
The famous Lyke Wake Walk, a long-distance footpath traverses the east to west watershed of the North York Moors through remote and mostly uninhabited moorland, passing Bronze Age burial mounds and lonely prehistoric standing stones (above) en route. The breathtaking view from Sutton Bank (left) on the western edge of the North York Moors was described by author James Herriot as the finest in England.

Fryup Dale

This quaintly-named corner of the North York Moors consists of two secluded valleys, Great and Little Fryup. Winding off the Esk valley, the area is unspoilt but even in May bitterly cold weather often blows down from the north-east and makes these valleys (above) difficult places to farm.

Glaisdale

The village of Glaisdale is a past winner of the "Village of the Year" award for the north of England. Even after a fall of snow (left) the fell high above the village is a majestic sight. The photograph was taken from the roadside near Low Gill Beck Farm, looking towards Glaisdale Moor.

Castleton

This linear village (left) sits on a high ridge where the rich secluded valleys of Westerdale and Danby Dale meet on the northern fringe of the Moors. The settlement is steeped in history. The village hall, built in 1869, was called the Temperance Hall until 15 years ago – a throwback to the days when temperance societies, aiming to discourage alcohol, existed in nearly every village. Castleton also has a Quaker graveyard.

Danby

This beautiful village (below) nestles at the western head of the Esk Valley and due to its high location was once part of a national network where beacons were lit at times of emergency. In the Second World War Danby was the site of a radar station that tracked incoming enemy planes. The very first enemy aircraft to be shot down during the war (by wartime hero Group Captain Peter Townsend) was tracked from Danby.

Roseberry Topping

On the border between the North York Moors and Cleveland, the distinctive half-coned shape of Roseberry Topping dominates much of the countryside around Guisborough. The hill's peculiar shape is due to the fact that half the summit has collapsed, owing to a geological fault or because many old alum or ironstone mines lie close to the top. On nearby Easby Moor there is an impressive monument to Captain Cook who went to school in nearby Great Ayton.

Mallyan Spout

The highest waterfall on the North York Moors, Mallyan Spout (above) near Goathland, cascades 60ft (18m) down the side of West Beck Gorge. A short walk alongside the beck just to the right of the Mallyan Spout Hotel leads to the waterfall. In wet weather, spray is blown across the path giving visitors the impression of walking through a waterfall.

Falling Foss

This picturesque waterfall (right) tumbles down a spectacular 30ft (9m) gorge close to the tiny hamlet of Little Beck, on a tributary of the Esk.

78

Rosedale

This is a long, extended valley which stretches out in a south-easterly direction from Westerdale Moor and Danby High Moor towards Hartoft End and Cropton Forest. The river Seven flows throughout its length and there are superb views across the dale from the road near the Lion Inn on Blakey Ridge. The Rosedale Show (above) is held every August in the delightful village of Rosedale Abbey. The picturesque church of St Lawrence (below) is at the heart of the village.

Goathland

This pretty village due north of Pickering is popular with visitors who are attracted by its *Heartbeat* association – in the series the village is the fictional Aidensfield. Goathland lies on the 24-mile stretch of the North York Moors Railway which runs from Pickering to Grosmont. The picturesque station (left) featured in *Harry Potter and the Philosopher's Stone*. Passengers heading north enjoy a superb view as the train makes a steep climb from Beck Hole and Darnworth. The parish church of St Mary's (above) is seen here on a crisp winter's day.

Old Byland

This tiny and peaceful hamlet (above) located just west of Rievaulx Abbey contains a few stone cottages and farm buildings surrounding a small village green. The church of All Saints with its distinctive high square porch dates from Norman times.

Hawnby

The church of All Saints (below) stands on the river Rye close to the remote settlement of Hawnby, a village of two halves separated by a steep hill. In the middle of the 18th century two villagers became the first Methodists in the neighbourhood. But the local landowner was very much opposed to their cause and the two men and their families were forced to resettle lower down in the valley close to the bridge, effectively splitting the village in two.

Farndale

This deep, narrow dale (left) is drained by the headwaters of the river Dove. It is a beautiful area with winding lanes and a patchwork of fields bounded by drystone walls. It is renowned for its spectacular spring displays of wild daffodils. It is estimated that about 35,000 people visit Farndale each year to see the daffodils, many using the specially designed "Daffodil Walk".

Hutton-le-Hole

Home to the Ryedale Folk Museum, this beautiful village (right) is a popular stopping-off point for visitors. Its broad village green, dotted with moorland sheep, is an ideal spot for a summer picnic. The Folk Museum, Yorkshire's leading open-air museum, has historic buildings depicting the past lives of north Yorkshire people.

Lastingham

A peaceful haven (below) nestling comfortably amidst glorious scenery, this is the ideal place to stroll and relax. Close by are attractions such as the Eden Camp Modern History Museum near Malton and the Flamingo Land theme park.

Lastingham Moor

Glorious moorland surrounds the peaceful village of Lastingham (above) which lies one and a half miles east of Hutton-le-Hole. The village has three unusual stone wells: one dedicated to St Cedd, a 7th century missionary from Lindisfarne, one to St Ovin and the last to St Chad. The beautiful church of St Mary is famous for its unique Norman crypt, which is the shrine to St Cedd who founded a monastery on the site.

Darnholm

These attractive stepping stones (left) cross the Eller Beck in the tiny hamlet of Darnholm one mile north of Goathland. The stepping stones are used by walkers and cars splash their way through the ford. This pretty spot is easily reached on foot from Goathland station. A fulling mill once occupied the valley bottom.

Rievaulx Abbey

Cistercian abbeys were usually situated in secluded locations; the site of Rievaulx Abbey in the depths of the narrow Rye valley must have provided the monks with a haven of peace and solitude. The ruins of the ancient abbey show that this was once one of the finest monastic churches in northern Britain. Fine views of the abbey can be enjoyed from the Rievaulx Terrace and Temples (right) which are situated on an escarpment high above the valley.

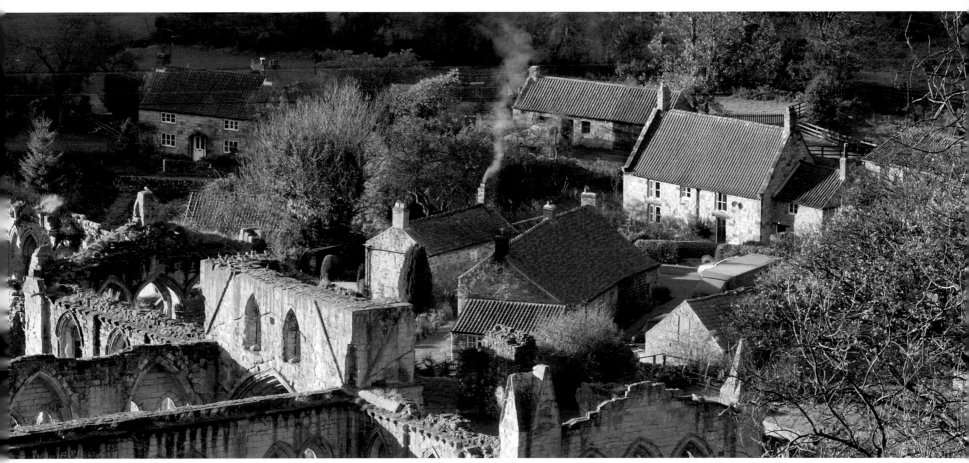

Hole of Horcum

Hollowed out of the heather-clad moor beside the Pickering to Whitby road, the Hole of Horcum is a huge natural amphitheatre. Legend has it that "the devil's punchbowl", as it is known locally, was created by a giant named Wade who scooped out the rocks and earth, tossing them two miles east to Blakey Topping. A popular circular walk from the roadside car park passes this derelict farm cottage (above) at Low Horcum.

Levisham

An attractive stop on the North York Moors Railway, Levisham nestles above the quiet and wooded winding valley of Newton Dale, seven miles north of Pickering. The small church of St John the Baptist (left) lies at the top of the village where the road and a footpath lead to the railway station in the bottom of the valley.

Sutton Bank

The Hambleton Escarpment rises abruptly to a height of around 1,000ft (305m), giving views (above) of more than 30 miles. Roulston Scar and Hood Hill lie to the left. Gormire Lake is lit by a dramatic sky stirred up by strong winds sweeping across the Vale of York.

The Cleveland Way

A short walk along the escarpment brings the visitor to Whitestone Cliff on the Cleveland Way footpath. The view here looks north towards Gormire Lake and Boltby. The 110-mile long Cleveland Way starts in the market town of Helmsley and traverses the upland ridge on the edge of the North York Moors before reaching the coast at Saltburn-by-the-Sea.

Pickering

This busy and elegant market town is located on the southern edge of the North York Moors. In the town centre is Beck Isle Museum of Rural Life. The museum transports visitors back through time as they pass through a wide variety of re-created settings including a cobbler's shop, blacksmith's, chemist, dairy and village store.

THE COAST

The eastern boundary of the North York Moors national park is known as the North Yorkshire Heritage Coast. This is a beautiful and varied area with high rugged cliffs, traditional fishing villages, small river inlets and wide sandy bays. The Heritage Coast includes the resorts of Sandsend, Runswick Bay, Whitby, Robin Hood's Bay and Ravenscar. Further south are the long-established holiday resorts of Scarborough, Filey, Bridlington, Hornsea and Withernsea, interspersed with some of the finest cliff scenery on the east coast of Britain at Flamborough Head and Bempton Cliffs.

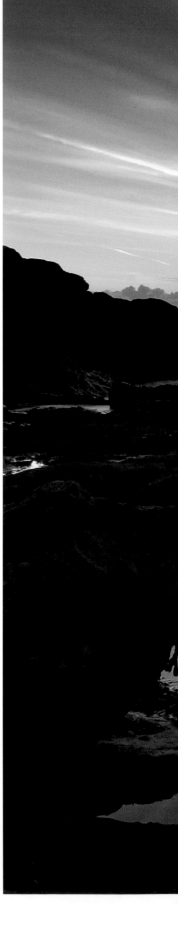

Runswick Bay and Cromer Point
Small wooden fishing boats called cobles (above) on the sandy beach at
Runswick Bay – one of the Heritage Coast's most beautiful villages.
Rockpools at Cromer Point, just north of Scarborough at first light (right).

Port Mulgrave

A tiny hamlet between Hinderwell and Staithes, Port Mulgrave (right) was developed in the 1850s when ironstone was mined locally. The harbour pier was specially constructed at this time but is now falling into disrepair as the North Sea takes its relentless toll.

Staithes

Beloved of artists and photographers, this quaint village (below) is in a dramatic setting on the rugged coastline north of Whitby. Known locally as "Steers" (due to the local dialect way of pronouncing its name), the village has a quaint cobbled harbour with a collection of white-painted cottages perched haphazardly around it. During the 1890s, the so-called Staithes Group of around 30 artists were active in the area, developing the best in British Impressionist painting.

Sandsend

This pretty village (left) is located at the foot of Lythe Bank where the sandy beach comes to an abrupt end. There are many picturesque cottages set against a backdrop of cliffs beside two meandering streams which flow out onto the beach. Sandsend is well known for its fossils and the majority are to be found at the northern end of the beach at the foot of Sandsend Ness.

Whitby

At the centre of what is often referred to as "Captain Cook Country", the seaside town of Whitby (above) has the only natural harbour between the Tees and the Humber and is where the young James Cook learned the seafarer's trade. The house in Grape Lane where he served his apprenticeship is now a museum. The town's skyline is dominated by the ruins of St Hilda's Abbey, high up on the east cliff next to the parish church of St Mary. The 199 steps that connect the parish church of St Mary (just visible in the photograph, left) to the town are a local institution. These "church stairs" were used to carry coffins up to the church; there are resting places for the pall-bearers to rest the coffin along the way.

Robin Hood's Bay

South of Whitby, this picturesque fishing village (right) has a series of winding streets and narrow alleyways (ginnels) lined with old houses and cottages, many with distinctive red pantiled roofs. In the 18th century, the bay was a centre for smuggling and there are a number of secret tunnels below the houses so that the smugglers could bring their illegal contraband ashore safely. From the surrounding countryside towards Ravenscar there are panoramic views (below) across the bay. The Coast to Coast long-distance trail devised by the famous fell-walker and writer Alfred Wainwright, which starts at St Bees on Cumbria's west coast, finally ends at Robin Hood's Bay. Weary walkers can sometimes be seen walking down the cobbled jetty to dip their sore feet in the sea. The trail is 190 miles long and participants typically take around 10-12 days to complete the trek.

Boggle Hole

For centuries Boggle Hole, just half a mile from Robin Hood's Bay, was a centre of smuggling. This small cove provided an easy and well-hidden base for landing goods, particularly under cover of darkness when the cargo could quickly be moved into the quiet surrounding countryside. Now you are more likely to find beachcombers of all ages exploring the rockpools for marine life and fossils. Access to the beach is relatively easy, with car parking half a mile from the clifftop and a delightful walk through woodland down to where the youth hostel lies just above the beach.

Ravenscar

One of the wildest and most exposed places on the Yorkshire coast, the steeply rising ground at Ravenscar (above) climbs to form a grassy plateau almost 600ft (182m) above sea level. Ravenscar is sometimes referred to as "the town that never was". In 1895, the Ravenscar Estate Company planned to build a new town here to challenge the nearby resorts of Whitby and Scarborough but the idea was abandoned due to the bitingly cold winds. There are fabulous views of Robin Hood's Bay from around the area, particularly from the coastal clifftop path, part of the Cleveland Way.

Scarborough

This elegant town is one of the north of England's most popular coastal towns and was Britain's first seaside resort. The ruined Norman castle and its headland (right) stand 150ft (46m) above the harbour and dominate Scarborough's skyline, dividing the town into North Bay and South Bay. One of the best views of the town and headland is from Oliver's Mount (below right) just above the town's spa complex

with its superb parks, theatres and conference hall. Dominating South Bay is the massive Grand Hotel; completed in 1867, at the time it was one of the largest hotels in the world. Its four towers represent the seasons and its 12 floors the months of the year. The Scarborough Cricket Festival is an end of season series of cricket matches featuring Yorkshire County Cricket Club played on the ground at North Marine Road (above). The matches have been played every year since 1876. Anne Brontë died in Scarborough at the age of 28 and is buried in the graveyard of St Mary's church.

Filey

Whilst neighbouring Scarborough and Bridlington grew rapidly into large seaside resorts in the mid-19th century, Filey developed a smaller tourist trade and depended on the income from its fishing fleet until fairly recently. Today, this elegant town with its fine beach and attractive centre offers quiet family-orientated holidays. The five-mile long sandy beach (below) at Filey is protected from the north by the magnificent Filey Brigg, a rocky promontory which extends over a mile into the North Sea. A marker on the cliffs above Filey Brigg marks the end of the Cleveland Way long-distance footpath. From Filey Brigg the semi-circular bay runs south to the chalk cliffs of Speeton and Bempton. This small and friendly town has many attractions including the coble landing where small fishing boats rest at jaunty angles outside the popular beachside cafe. There is a week-long Edwardian festival every year in June, where residents and shopkeepers dress up in period costume; the magnificent prominent row of Victorian houses called the Crescent is just one example of Filey's fine architecture.

Great Givendale and Muston

The small village of Givendale, on the edge of the Yorkshire Wolds, is home to the tiny church of St Ethelburga (left). Set within deciduous woodland, it is particularly lovely in spring when the snowdrops and primroses are in flower. In the winter's scene (below left) All Saints church at Muston, near Filey, can be seen blanketed in snow. The Yorkshire Wolds Way, which runs from Hessle on the Humber estuary to Filey passes close to both villages.

Burnby Hall

This beautiful house and gardens (below right) near the centre of Pocklington is home to the National Collection of Water Lillies. The site contains over 80 varieties of water lily, the largest collection in the world. The plants can be seen at their best in July and August when they are in bloom. The collection is the work of Major Stewart Percy, a real-life Indiana Jones figure, who owned Burnby Hall and collected the specimens during seven world tours between 1906 and 1926. The Stewart Museum in the grounds describes his life and displays artefacts collected during his tours.

Bempton

At the southern end of Filey Bay, Bempton Cliffs (above and right) were bought by the RSPB in 1969 and is one of the best known nature reserves for seabirds in the UK. Throughout the year more than a quarter of a million birds nest here. Puffin, guillemot and kittiwake abound on the cliffs and a major attraction is the huge gannet colony – the only nesting site for these birds on the British mainland. Access for visitors is easy by car or on foot from the little village of Bempton, one mile inland. The best time to see the seabirds is during the nesting season from June to August, although visitors can enjoy bracing walks along the cliffs and visit the RSPB visitor centre throughout the year.

Flamborough

The coastline at Flamborough Head (above) is one of the most spectacular areas of chalk cliff in Britain. Dramatic cliffs, some reaching 400ft (122m), thrust up out of the sea, providing a haven for wildlife. Thornwick Bay is just one of the many sheltered, shingle coves fronting the sea with caves and dramatic stacks. The old Beacon lighthouse at Flamborough was first built in 1674. The new lighthouse was built in 1806 by John Matson of Bridlington.

Sewerby

Close to the tiny hamlet of Sewerby, large lumps of boulder clay at the base of the cliffs show how the coast is being eroded by wind and sea. The photograph (right) looks from the rocky beach in front of the cliffs towards Bridlington, two miles to the south.

Hornsea

A small seaside resort situated 16 miles north of Hull and 14 miles south of Bridlington, Hornsea has an attractive town centre with houses dating back to the 15th century. The attractive cobblestone parish church of St Nicholas (right), close to the centre, was built in the 14th century. The town's best known attraction is the Mere, a 465-acre freshwater lake which is the largest natural lake in Yorkshire. A marker on the seafront marks one end of the Trans-Pennine Trail which finishes in Southport in Lancashire. Part of the trail is along the track of the old railway line built in 1851 to link Hornsea to Hull.

On the southern edge of the town is the site of the famous pottery first set up in 1949 by Desmond and Colin Rawson. The resort is fringed by attractive pebble and sandy beaches (below) and there is a newly developed promenade. From the seafront there are spectacular views to Spurn Head and the entrance to the Humber estuary.

Bridlington

With two glorious long sandy beaches, miles of elegant promenades and a very pretty and bustling harbour (above) Bridlington has all the ingredients for the perfect holiday resort. Flamborough Head and its lighthouse are clearly visible from the north pier and beach. The town is divided into two parts, the old town about a mile inland which originated around the abbey at Bridlington Priory and the holiday resort and fishing port at the quay fringing Bridlington Bay. Bridlington's first hotel was opened in 1805 and it soon became a popular resort for the city dwellers of West Yorkshire. The Beside the Seaside Exhibition close to the harbour contains fascinating exhibits of the town in its heyday.

Beverley

This ancient town, eight miles north of Hull, has held a large market (right) since medieval times. Local courts keen to boost the number of buyers and ensure that the market had a sound and reliable reputation were quick to fine any trader who sold short measures. The town is packed with historic buildings including the Guildhall which has a fine 18th century courthouse. The well-known racecourse is located high above the town on historic Westwood, a large piece of common ground, west of the town centre.

Burton Agnes Hall

This beautiful Elizabethan hall (below) lies halfway between Driffield and Bridlington in the village of Burton Agnes. The building is packed with paintings, furniture and porcelain and the Long Gallery, running the entire length of the top floor, and the Great Hall are regarded as masterpieces of Jacobean architecture. The walled garden and maze are a favourite with visitors.

Beverley Minster

The beautiful parish church of St John and St Martin, generally known as Beverley Minster, is regarded as one of the most impressive Gothic buildings in Europe. The slender twin towers of the minster can be seen throughout the town and its approaches. The church was built between 1220 and 1435 around the tomb of Saint John, the medieval saint who founded a monastery in the town. Long before the church was built, the tomb became an important place of pilgrimage, helping to make Beverley a prosperous town. Such was the cult built up around John that Edward I regularly visited his tomb to pray for good fortune on his way north to fight the Scots. Henry V attributed his victory at Agincourt to divine intervention by the saint.

Withernsea

The pier towers (right) along the seafront at Withernsea were once the grand entrance to a 1,200ft (365m) long pier built in 1877. Over the years the pier suffered severe damage after collisions with ships and the decision was finally taken in the 1930s to remove the remaining stump. The towers are now the grand entrance to an attractive sandy beach. The town's most unusual attraction is the white inland lighthouse – now no longer active – on Hull Road.

Spurn Head

Situated on the north bank of the entrance to the river Humber, this three-mile long finger of land that snakes out into the Humber estuary is constantly being reshaped by storms and coastal erosion. The distinctive black-and-white lighthouse (below) became redundant in 1985 and has now been replaced by automatic beacons.

Humber Bridge

Opened in 1981, this beautiful suspension bridge (above) was built to link north Lincolnshire and Humberside across the wide Humber estuary. Almost 1.5 miles long, the bridge has cut 50 miles off the road journey between the major ports of Hull and Grimsby. The south tower of the bridge is founded in shallow water 1,650ft (500m) from the shore.

Hull

The gleaming glass and aluminium marine life centre – The Deep – opened in 2002 and symbolises the regeneration of this city which was once a centre of whaling and deep-sea fishing. The Deep stands at the confluence of the rivers Hull and Humber and was conceived to educate and inform its visitors about the world's oceans. Although its fishing industry has declined, Hull, or Kingston-upon-Hull, to give it its full name, is still a major port handling large amounts of general cargo and being the base for ferry routes to Rotterdam and Zeebrugge. The Maritime Museum (right), formerly the Town Docks Museum, is housed in an impressive building constructed in 1867-71 as the dock offices. Built in the Venetian Renaissance style, it overlooks the former Queen's Dock. The leaded domes on the building are topped by lanterns supported by dolphins. The museum has displays on whaling, an important collection of scrimshaw and a section outlining the roles of Hull trawlers in both world wars. Anchored in the Marina is the Spurn Lightship (left). This light vessel (a floating light-house) was built in 1927 and served for 48 years as an aid to navigation anchored several miles to the east of Spurn Point. It is now a museum.

101

SOUTH YORKSHIRE

South Yorkshire ranges from high, bleak moorlands in the west, covered in heather and blanket bog, without a sign of habitation, through the densely populated Coal Measure country containing the city of Sheffield and the towns of Barnsley and Rotherham, to the fertile agricultural country of the Magnesian Limestone belt, and then stretches beyond Doncaster to the east to the Humberhead Levels only a few feet above sea level. It is a many-layered landscape created by the endeavours of people using its resources over many thousands of years to make a living and create farmsteads, villages and urban and industrial settlements, large and small. Yet this densely populated region contains many architectural and landscape gems, in particular, fine medieval, 18th century and Victorian buildings, public parks and country houses with their surrounding parks and gardens. In the west there are large sweeps of open country and elsewhere tracts of attractive walled, hedged and wooded farmed countryside.

Peace Gardens, Sheffield & the Pennine Moors
Crowds of people enjoy a sunny summer's day in Sheffield's Peace Gardens (above), a welcome green open space right in the heart of the city and (right) in complete contrast, in the extreme west of the region, uninhabited moorlands, at their highest exceeding 1,800ft (550m) above sea level, cut through by the headwaters of the Derwent and the Don and its tributaries.

Sheffield Town Hall

The centre of Sheffield is dominated by the Town Hall, built of Derbyshire sandstone, standing at the junction of Surrey Street and Pinstone Street. Designed by EW Mountford, it was described by Sir Nikolaus Pevsner as "a large picturesque pile". It was opened by Queen Victoria in 1897, who was greeted by Sheffield's first lord mayor, the Duke of Norfolk. Two friezes carved in stone adorn the exterior walls; they depict, among other things, grinders, smiths, smelters and miners. The 200ft tower (left) is surmounted by an 8ft high bronze statue of Vulcan, the Roman god of fire and furnaces, with his right foot on an anvil and pincers in his left hand. Inside is a life-size statue of the Duke of Norfolk and a bust of Queen Victoria. Another striking building is the Methodist's Victoria Hall (right) in Norfolk Street. Built in brick and stone in a mixture of Gothic and Arts & Crafts styles it was completed in 1908. It has a landmark tower with a massive Baroque top and interesting carved decoration.

High Street, Sheffield

Leading from the site of the castle and the market area towards the parish church (now the cathedral), High Street has always been an important commercial street since the founding of a town in Norman times. In the right background can be seen Kemsley House, the Sheffield Telegraph building, completed in 1916 and faced with white faience. In the left foreground is the former John Walsh's department store, which was rebuilt after the Second World War to replace the original store opened in 1899 but destroyed in the Blitz in 1940. The Supertram is on its way to the Meadowhall Shopping Centre with 270 stores and parking for 12,000 cars.

Sheffield's parks & gardens

The first of Sheffield's public open spaces, the Botanical Gardens (above) opened in 1836. It was a forerunner of nearly a dozen public parks that would encircle the city like pearls on a necklace. A competition was held to obtain a design for the gardens, the glass pavilions, entrance and lodges. Robert Marnock won first prize, was appointed curator and laid out the gardens in fashionable "gardenesque" style. In 1997 the Botanical Gardens received a £5m award from the Heritage Lottery Fund leading to complete restoration of the gardens and pavilions to their former splendour. The latest addition to Sheffield's public green spaces is the Winter Garden (right), opened in December 2002. It houses 150 species of plants mainly from the northern hemisphere. Underfloor heating protects the plants from frost.

Sheffield Cathedral

The church of St Peter and St Paul (right), Sheffield's medieval parish church, became Sheffield cathedral in 1914. The present church initially dates from the early 15th century, replacing an earlier church probably of early 12th century origin. The crossing tower surmounted by its crocketed spire is an important local landmark. The Shrewsbury Chapel contains the tombs of the 4th Earl of Shrewsbury (died 1538) lying between his two wives and the 6th Earl of Shrewsbury (died 1590) with his feet resting on a Talbot, a hunting dog bearing the family name. In the churchyard is a monument to James Montgomery (1771-1854), newspaper editor and proprietor, anti-slavery campaigner, poet and hymn writer. He wrote more than 350 hymns, the best known being *Angels from the Realms of Glory*.

Bradfield Moors

The physical setting of Sheffield is equalled by no other British city. It is enveloped in the west by very extensive tracts of high moorland and upland pastures rising to more than 1,800ft (550m), all within the modern city boundaries and much of it part of the Peak District National Park. No moorland can be bleaker or more beautiful, according to the season, than the Bradfield Moors which stretch westwards from Bradfield village beyond Agden Reservoir reaching in their highest parts to more than 1,500ft (457m).

Bradfield village

There are in fact two villages, Low Bradfield and High Bradfield. Dominating High Bradfield is St Nicholas' parish church, one of the largest churches in Hallamshire. The churchyard contains some very old gravestones but most interesting is one dating from 1864 when the nearby Dale Dyke Reservoir burst its banks and the rushing torrent of water, pouring down the Loxley valley towards Sheffield, resulted in the death of 240 people. The gravestone in question is that of James Trickett, his wife and three children who all perished in the flood and the last two lines of the dedication reads: "Whate'er the fault this is most true, The Flood is a warning to me and to you." At the entrance to the churchyard is what is reputed to have been a watch-house (above right) built as a lookout point to discourage body-snatchers!

Barnsley Town Hall

Barnsley's Town Hall, sited at the junction of Church Street and Shambles Street at the top of Market Hill, was erected when Barnsley was still the coal capital of South Yorkshire and still dominates the townscape today. Constructed in 1932-33, of white limestone blocks, it was designed by the Liverpool architects, Briggs & Thornely. It replaced the dingy old Town Hall in St Mary's Gate. Its imposing frontage, 21 bays long, is surmounted by a conspicuous clock tower. But it may not have ever had a clock tower – it was omitted from the final design on financial grounds and consent by the town council for its construction was only given at the last minute, four months after the foundation stone was laid. The cost of building and furnishing came to £188,000, an enormous figure in the depression days of the 1930s.

Wentworth Castle

Wentworth Castle is not a castle and not at Wentworth but at Stainborough. The hall consists of a north-west facing wing built by Sir Gervase Cutler between 1670-72 together with a north-east facing wing in the Baroque style (below) which was finished in the 1720s and a Palladian-style front facing south-east elevation built between 1759-64. In 1948 the house, outbuildings and 60 acres of garden were bought by Barnsley Education Committee. In 1949 it opened as a teacher training college and in 1978 became Northern College. The grounds of the house hold a Grade 1 listing. It featured in the BBC Television's *Restoration* series. A special feature of the gardens is a recently renovated mock medieval castle – Stainborough Castle (left).

Rotherham

Rotherham's origins lie beside an important river crossing, of the river Don, first as a ford and then as a bridge, below its confluence with the river Rother. The bridge chapel (left) is one of only four bridge chapels still surviving in England. Constructed in Rotherham Red sandstone, it was built in the late 15th century and travellers could give thanks for their safe arrival in the town or pray for a safe journey on departure. After the Reformation the chapel was converted into almshouses and then became the town jail and a private residence. By the beginning of the 20th century, much to the dismay of many of Rotherham's citizens, it was used as a tobacconist's shop. The tobacconist was bought out in 1913 and the chapel was handed over to the Church Commissioners and re-consecrated by the Bishop of Sheffield in 1924. The old town grew up on the eastern bank of the river where a low bluff provided a commanding site for All Saints parish church (right) rebuilt at the end of the Middle Ages in the Perpendicular style. This has dominated the town ever since. It is generally regarded as one the most magnificent parish churches in Yorkshire. Inside it has a beautiful panelled nave and chancel ceilings with bosses, and a memorial to 50 people, many of them children, who drowned when a canal barge was being launched in 1841.

Clifton House Museum

Clifton House Museum (below), in Clifton Park, dates from the 1780s and was originally the home of Joshua Walker, son of Samuel Walker, one of the founders of Masbrough Iron Foundry. It is believed that the house was designed by John Carr, the York architect. The Council paid £25,000 for Clifton House and 54 acres of surrounding parkland in 1891 "for the use of the townspeople in perpetuity". It became a museum in 1893. The opening of Clifton Park took place on 25 June, 1891 and it was a splendid royal, and, it must be said, hilarious occasion in part. The official opening was conducted by the Prince and Princess of Wales (later King Edward VII and Queen Alexandra).

Also present, as the leading local figure, was the mayor of Rotherham, Alderman Neill, bedecked in his newly acquired cocked hat and mayoral chain of office (made by local jeweller John Mason). The mayor must have looked particularly regal to the local juvenile population because when he and his wife arrived at the park ahead of the royal party and stepped down from their carriage, 10,000 children on specially erected stands mistook him for the royal personage and began to sing their well-rehearsed song God Bless the Prince of Wales to "considerable merriment".

After Rotherham became a metropolitan borough in 1974 it was

clear that the old Town Hall on Howard Street was too small and when new court buildings were opened and the court house in the Crofts (right) became vacant it was converted into a new Town Hall, opened in 1995.

Roche Abbey

Roche Abbey was founded in 1147 on a site given by two patrons, Richard de Busli and Richard Fitzurgis. It is a typical Cistercian site, tucked away in a secluded spot with a good water supply. Although only an inner gatehouse and the church transepts (left) reach to any height, a complete Cistercian abbey plan is exposed in the ruins. In the 1770s Capability Brown was employed by the owner, the Earl of Scarborough, to landscape the site and he covered up and planted over the ruins of the abbey. These have now been fully exposed to reveal the full abbey site.

Wentworth Woodhouse

The mansion that can be seen from the park at Wentworth (above) is the East or Palladian front. It was begun by Thomas Watson-Wentworth (later the Marquis of Rockingham) in 1732. It superseded another house facing west built in the florid Baroque style. The Palladian front extends to a length of 606ft (183m), the longest country house front in England. From the village of Wentworth the park is entered beside the Octagon Lodge, one of five surviving lodges. Some visitors entering the park for the first time from this direction are so impressed by the stable block with its clock tower (right) that they think that it is the mansion! The deer park is the only remaining deer park in South Yorkshire that still contains deer. The 100-strong herd can often be glimpsed grazing among the trees that are scattered throughout the park.

Conisbrough Castle

This magnificent stone castle stands aloft on a tiny "island" of Magnesian Limestone, controlling an important crossing point on the river Don. Dominating all is the stone keep, a massive cylindrical tower, nearly 99ft (30m) high with walls 15ft (4.6m) thick. Attached to the basic cylinder shape are six splayed buttresses which rise to become turrets. By Elizabethan times the castle was in disrepair and was never garrisoned during the Civil War of the 1640s. This saved it from destruction. Now the floors of the keep have been reinstated and the conical roof is once more in place.

St George, Doncaster

Completed in 1858, this minster church was designed by Sir George Gilbert Scott to replace the medieval St Mary's, destroyed in a fire in 1853. It has a fine Perpendicular tower, a virtual replica of the one lost in the fire. The interior is big: it is about 170ft (52m) long and the nave 75ft (23m) tall and it is richly decorated. Its fine Victorian stained glass includes a 39ft (10m) high east window.

Cusworth Hall and Park

William Wrightson (1676-1760) was the owner responsible for the building of the hall that stands today. The Rotherham mason-architect, George Platt, began to supervise the building of the new hall and on his death in 1742, his son, John, took over. Later extensions were designed by James Paine, the Palladian-style architect. William Wrightson's son-in-law, John Battie-Wrightson, commissioned Richard Woods, the landscape gardener, to improve the 100 acres of grounds surrounding the new hall between 1750-53. Features of the landscaped park dating from this period include three lakes, a bridge, a grotto-like boathouse and a cascade. The park and the house now belong to Doncaster Metropolitan Borough Council, the house having become a museum in 1967. The house and park underwent restoration between 2004-07 partly funded by a £4.9m Heritage Lottery grant.

Cusworth Hall Chapel

As part of the recent Heritage Lottery-funded refurbishment, the roofs of the hall have been replaced and the stonework repaired. Inside the original colour schemes have been reverted to and even the doors have been restored to their original style and colour. Perhaps the most stunning restoration work can be seen in the chapel which was built between 1750 and 1755 under the direction of James Paine. Paine wrote to Wrightson to say that he had "designed the chapel in very gentiel taste..." Among craftsmen employed were Joseph Rose, the stuccoist and the artist Francis Hayman, once a student of Hogarth. Hayman is recorded as being "paid in full – £25/5/0 for his work in the Chappel". He painted *The Good Samaritan*, placed over a communion table of which a copy still survives (left) and on the vaulted ceiling *The Ascension* (below).

Brodsworth Hall

South Yorkshire has a rich heritage of country houses, parks and gardens. Brodsworth Hall, five miles north-west of Doncaster, is a fine Italianate-style country house, of Magnesian Limestone, built and furnished between 1861-63 for Charles Sabine Augustus Thellusson. The house and grounds remained in family ownership until 1990 when they were acquired by English Heritage. After a five-year programme of restoration and conservation they were opened to the public in 1995. The house was designed by Chevalier Casentini. As far as is known Casentini never came to South Yorkshire and his designs were executed by a little-known architect called Philip Wilkinson. From the entrance hall there is a magnificent sequence of halls on the ground floor with painted marbling on the walls and *scagliola* (imitation marble) columns and pilasters. Silhouetted against the dark walls are the white marble, mostly female, figures (15 large ones and eight small ones) of Charles Thelluson's collection of Italian sculptures purchased in 1865. The west stairs takes the visitor to the bedrooms on the first floor and beyond to the servants' wing. Neat lawns surround the house which sits on a raised terrace of grass banks. At intervals are steps embellished with marble urns (*tazzas*) and greyhounds. Behind the house are croquet lawns (above) and beyond them 15 acres of gardens. The gardens include a large formal garden of symmetrical beds, with stunning bedding schemes, cut out of the turf in shapes said to have been unchanged since they were laid out in the 1860s (right), statues and sculptures, a quarry garden with ferns including the giant tree fern *Dicksonia antarctica*, an Italianate summerhouse, and the "Target House", a small garden building in a rustic Swiss style, all linked by walks lined with clipped shrubs.

Fishlake Church

St Cuthbert's, the medieval church in Fishlake, a small village on the flatlands to the north-east of Doncaster, is mainly in the Perpendicular style. It is reputedly dedicated to St Cuthbert because monks carried the remains of St Cuthbert, a hermit monk, from the Farne Islands around northern England for several years to keep them out of the hands of the Viking raiders, and Fishlake is supposed to be one of the places where his remains rested for a period. The south doorway of the church (above), all that remains of the Norman church that once stood on the site, is probably the most lavishly carved medieval church doorway in Yorkshire.

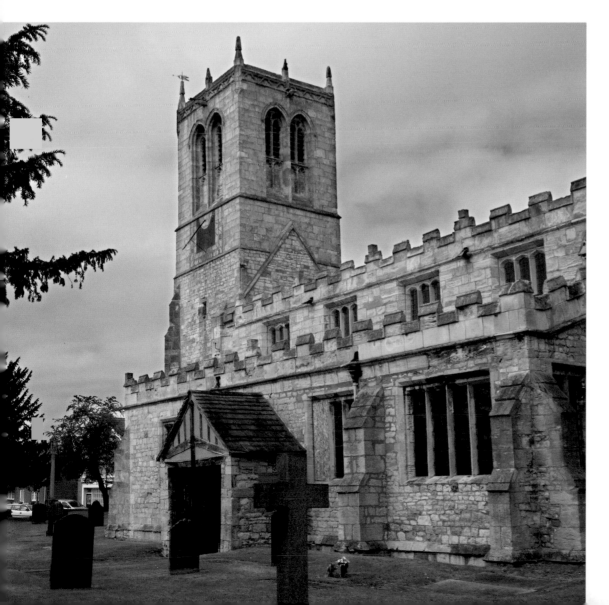

Sprotbrough

Sprotbrough stands on a hillside overlooking the river Don just a few miles south-west of Doncaster. A focal point for visitors is the waterside at the foot of the hill. Here the canal, which runs alongside the river, has been dredged and deepened and an electric lock has been installed. The canal was once heavily used, coal and limestone being important cargoes, but now only pleasure boats use the canal. The iron bridge replaced a ferry crossing between the village and Warmsworth in 1888. Yorkshire Wildlife Trust has created a nature reserve, the Sprotbrough Flash, at a subsidence lake on the valley floor which is attractive to many waterside birds.

Sprotbrough Church

The oldest parts of St Mary's, Sprotbrough, date from the late 13th century. The solid tower was heightened in the Perpendicular period when William Fitzwilliam, who died in 1474, left £40 for the work. There are fine brasses to William and his wife on the chancel floor. The church has stone effigies of a late 13th century knight, a 14th century lady and of Philip Copley (who died in 1577) and his wife. There is also "a mysterious stone seat", the so-called "Frith Stool" with 14th century carvings.

125

Tickhill

Tickhill is perhaps the most pleasant small town in South Yorkshire. The centre of the town has the air of an ancient market town unaffected by industrialisation. This atmosphere is enhanced by the fact that the town centre has two rookeries and the churchyard is carpeted with celandines in early spring. Yet Tickhill did not grow naturally from an ancient village into a market town – it was an artificial foundation, a planned medieval town established by its Norman lord to serve his estate and his main residence, Tickhill castle. The name Tickhill is derived from the name "Tica's hill", a natural hill that formed the bottom part of the motte on which the Norman castle was built.

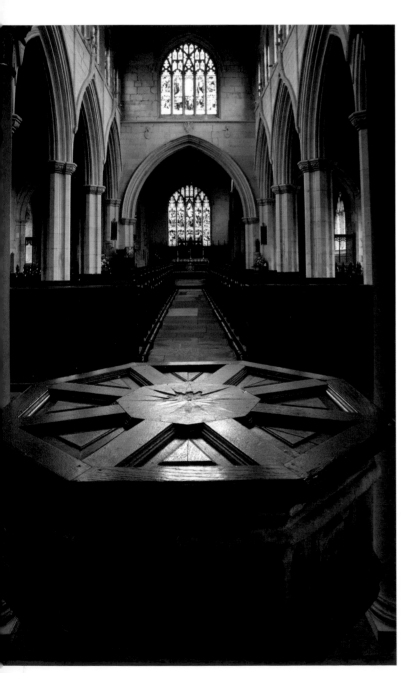

St Mary's

Tickhill is now dominated by St Mary's parish church, one of the outstanding Perpendicular churches in South Yorkshire. It is built of Magnesian Limestone and both inside (far left) and outside (left) can only be described as stately. It contains magnificent stone tombs (above), stone coffins, iron-bound wooden chests and medieval stained glass. Two other unusual buildings are the market or butter cross (top right) and St Leonard's Hospital, a timber-framed building dating from 1478 (bottom right). The hospital was founded as a leper hospital in 1225 and its original site was probably in the marshes to the east of the town.

Bawtry

Bawtry rivals Tickhill in its attractiveness and the reason is the same: it was bypassed by modern industrialisation and central redevelopment. It also shares with Tickhill a planned medieval origin. The planned town was laid out towards the end of the 12th century to reap the benefits of the river trade on the river Idle at the junction of the Great North Road and the highway westwards to Sheffield and Rotherham. To the east along the river Idle lay access to the rivers Trent and Humber, and beyond to the North Sea and the continent. The river trade declined with improvements to the Don but Bawtry's location on the Great North Road meant that it could take full advantage of increased

road travel in the turnpike era and it became a leading coaching town. St Nicholas' parish church (St Nicholas is the patron saint of seafarers) is on the eastern edge of the planned town near the former river wharf. Few vestiges of the river port have survived but notable exceptions are the late 17th century Dutch House at the corner of Church Street and Wharf Street with its swirling Dutch gables suggesting trading links with the Low Countries and the Ship Inn at the southern end of Church Street on the site of an earlier inn. The coaching era gave Bawtry much of its present character especially along High Street, around the Market Place and on South Parade. Here the coaching inn, The Crown, handsome Georgian houses and elegant terraces have survived.